CREWE AND NANTWICH

A Pictorial History

Borough of Crewe and Nantwich. Armorial Bearings, 1974. The red and gold quartered shield used by both Nantwich Urban District and Rural District Councils is that of the Malbank family which held these lands in Norman times. The old borough of Crewe is commemorated in the locomotive engine wheel, while the three wheat sheaves signify the amalgamation of three local authorities. Represented by wavy roundels are the rivers Weaver and Waldron, and the griffins' red and gold collars denote the ancient families of Audley, Delves and Fouleshurst. The griffins themselves were the supporters of both the Crewe and Cholmondeley family shields.

CREWE AND NANTWICH

A Pictorial History

Richard Simpson

Phillimore

1991

Published by
PHILLIMORE & CO. LTD.
Shopwyke Hall, Chichester, Sussex

ISBN 0 85033 724 0

Printed and bound in Great Britain by
BIDDLES LTD.,
Guildford, Surrey

For my sisters Joan and Barbara, and my brothers-in-law William and Norman:
the Cheshire branch of the family

List of Illustrations

Frontispiece: Armorial Bearings for the Borough of Crewe and Nantwich, 1974

Buildings and Streets

Industry and Agriculture

Transport

Acknowledgements

I am grateful to those authors who have gone before and for Dr. Diane K. Drummond's thesis on Crewe's development. Several books on railway history were needed to assess the technical details of L.N.W.R. locomotives and their working. Mr. G. R. Pimlett, Principal Librarian at Crewe, supplied a book list and arranged for photographs from the local history section to be copied. His staff also assisted my researches. My brother-in-law, Norman Rowlinson, provided many useful contacts, in particular with Harold Finch, programme secretary of Crewe Alexandra AFC; Harry Lindop, captain at Crewe Golf Club; and David Preston, public relations officer of Rolls Royce Motor Cars Ltd. Harry Lindop, a third generation worker at the Railway Works, gave generously of his time to provide 'an insider's view' of the works in the 1940s.

Any historian of the town must be grateful that Albert Hunn took so many photographs of Crewe before the redevelopment of 1960-70.

Finally, I thank those staff of my publisher Phillimore & Co., Chichester, without whom the task could not have been completed: Frances Mee, Noel Osborne and Val White.

Photographic material was supplied by the following: Cheshire Record Office (by permission of Principal Cheshire College of Agriculture), 67, 123, 168, 174; Crewe Alexandra Football Club, 126; Crewe Library, 1, 3, 4, 9, 10, 12-14, 17, 52, 59, 73, 75, 76, 88, 89 130, 141-143; Crewe and Nantwich Borough Council, frontispiece; Mrs. M. Fewtrell, 53; Mrs. H. Lindrop senior, 51; Nantwich Library, 2, 16, 18, 19, 28-31, 38, 70, 90-92, 105, 115, 118, 120, 124, 125, 127, 136, 137, 140, 149, ,150, 153-157, 171, 172; Nantwich Museum (by permission of the trustees), 34, 37, 93, 116, 122, 139, 151, 152; National Railway Museum (by permission of the Director), 7, 41-50, 54, 73, 74, 78-87, 100, 101, 103, 127-129, 131; Rector of St Bertoline's church, 161; Martyn Riley, 5, 64, 65, 94; Rolls Royce Motor Cars Ltd., 55-58, 60-63, 132-135; Vicar of St Mary's church, 165, 169; Vicar of St Boniface's church, 163, 164; Messrs Youngs Books, Nantwich Station, 77, 102, 104, 147.

The rest of the photographs were taken specially for the book by the author and copyright remains with him.

Any errors and/or omissions remain my responsibility.

Introduction

The twin settlements of Crewe and Nantwich lie centrally in the Cheshire Plain at the hub of the Midland Gap, separated by a mere four miles. Though both names appear in Domesday Book, Nantwich enjoyed early success as an urban centre, and Earl Edwin may have had a hall in neighbouring Acton as early as Saxon times. Ancient routeways from Chester, North Wales and North West England converged at Nantwich. In the 17th and 18th centuries canals developed around the town, whereas Crewe was bypassed by such transport. Welsh cattle were traded for salt in medieval days, and Irish goods transhipped at Chester passed through Nantwich on their way south. The earliest record of a market dates from 1283 when the king granted a right of fair on the feast of St Bartholomew. Cheese, grain, livestock and salt were traded in the town. Cheshire cheese has been famed from these times, being produced in farmhouses throughout the rich agricultural belt from Malpas in the south of the county through Nantwich and Tarporley to the Vale of Chester. Tanning was established in the town from medieval days, and glovemaking was an ancient cottage industry practised by 'poor incapable of following any other employ'.

All this was to change when the decision to move the railway workshops of the Grand Junction Railway from Edge Hill, Liverpool, to Crewe was taken in the late 1830s. From this date canals were used less and less for trade; today their sole use is for leisure pursuits. It is significant that the London and North Western Railway route to the North and South was completed with the acquisition of the Grand Junction Railway in 1846, only 11 years after the completion of the Birmingham and Liverpool Junction canal, the last great cross-country canal to be developed in the U.K. Ironically, trade continued on the canal system into Wales when the L.N.W.R. leased these routeways from the Shropshire Union Railways and Canal Company as from 1849. In this way the L.N.W.R. was able to penetrate Great Western Railway territory without the necessity of laying expensive railroads into this sparsely populated border country. Canals thus leased continued to show a profit until the early decades of the 20th century. The L.N.W.R. even developed a new inland port at Ellesmere Port near which the Chester canal entered the Mersey Estuary. Today this houses the Boat Museum.

The earliest written records of Nantwich appear as a series of entries in Domesday Book, when Cheshire was being assessed for taxation purposes by the servants of William the Conqueror. The lands of Hugh Lupus, Earl of Chester, were assessed thus: 'In Wich there are 7 salthouses which belonged to this manor; one of them pays salt to the hall; the others are disused'. The tenant of the earl's salthouse was William Malbeng, Lord of Wych Malbeng (the ancient name of the town). A salthouse consisted of 12 salt pans in which spring brine was evaporated to produce salt of greater purity than that gained by evaporating seawater. For this reason, Cheshire salt was highly prized both as seasoning and to preserve meat and fish through the winter period. It was jealously guarded as a source of revenue through taxation by local lords and king alike. In the 13th century, tolls were levied by the 'horseload' and the 'cartload', demonstrating the considerable trade involved.

Recent excavations at Wood Street have discovered that a salthouse could produce 100 gallons of salt at a boiling. In Nantwich Hundred the scale of charges was determined by whether the trader was an inhabitant of the hundred or a stranger. The acme of the salt trade in Nantwich was reached in the 16th century and decline set in from then until 1856 when the industry finally succumbed to the availability of easily mined rock salt of Northwich. Old practices and archaic regulations proved too expensive by comparison. Nevertheless, Nantwich remained second only to Chester until the industrial revolution led to the rapid rise of Stockport in East Cheshire.

The Great Fire of 1583 helps to estimate the approximate size of the town, since 600 timber-framed properties in the heart of the town were destroyed by the fire which raged unabated for 20 days. The scale of the disaster can be judged by the losses of some £30,000, a huge sum at contemporary prices. Queen Elizabeth was so appalled that she contributed £2,000 to rebuilding costs and decreed that timber should be cut from the Royal Forest of Delamere nearby. At this time Crewe was just a rural area with a few farms, the largest settlement here being the village of Barthomley.

The parish registers of St Mary, Nantwich, reveal that plague reached the town in 1586 when 140 persons were buried. In 1604, 430 people died from plague which persisted for six months. Rural Crewe escaped such catastrophes until the middle decades of the 19th century when inadequate water supplies and primitive sewage disposal led to outbreaks of cholera in the cramped artisan dwellings of both towns.

The Puritans were active in the vicinity of Nantwich in Elizabethan days. John and Thomas Paget were notable lecturers in the town during the reign of James I. Edward Burghall, vicar of Bunbury and later of Acton, on the return of King Charles II was expelled from the living at Acton for his Puritan preaching. Maybe such men as these alerted ordinary folk to the existence of nonconformity, for South Cheshire was strongly for Parliament during the Civil War. A Parliamentary force under the command of Major Lothian expelled a Royalist contingent from the town on 28 January 1643 when a company of horse under Lord Aston fled in confusion as darkness fell, in the First Battle of Nantwich. A minor Cheshire squire, Sir William Brereton of Handforth, commanded the Parliamentary forces in Cheshire from his headquarters in the *Lamb* Hotel. He had soon realised the strategic position of Nantwich which could block any relieving Royalist forces if they disembarked from Ireland at Chester and sought to make their way south. In the Cheshire campaign of 1643-6 he was able to fortify the town with small forts and earthworks, known as sconces, which sealed off the ends of strategic streets. Sconces were built across Beam Street, Frog Row, Pillory Street, Hospital Street and Wall Lane so that all entry points were closely defended.

Nantwich was besieged by Royalist forces but never fell, becoming the only Cheshire town held continuously for Parliament, with 2,000 troops garrisoned in the town. Middlewich was attacked on 13 March 1643 and foot soldiers from Nantwich were involved in this successful affray. Brereton also led expeditions against Warrington, Wem and Stafford from his Nantwich stronghold. The Royalist Eastern Army, under Lord Byron, attacked the town on 25 January 1644 (the Second Battle of Nantwich). However, their picket covering the bridge was thrust aside by troops of the Parliamentary garrison who then attacked the Royal force in the flank. Thus the Royalists were soundly defeated and the siege of the town was raised. Dorfold Hall at Acton was used as the Royalist headquarters on this occasion.

One thousand five hundred prisoners taken at the battle were detained in St Mary's, Nantwich, including Colonel George Monk, an important Royalist commander who later changed his allegiance to Parliament. This same church was used to contain 900 Scottish prisoners after the defeat of the Duke of Hamilton at Preston in the 1648 campaign. It was not just soldiery who damaged the church fabric – complaints in later days were made about the carvings of pupils from Acton Grammar School who worshipped at St Mary's, Acton.

Nonconformity gained root at Nantwich from the 18th century. The Friends Meeting House dates from 1724, whilst the Unitarians erected a chapel in Pratchitt's Row in 1726. Perhaps their most famous minister was Joseph Priestley, scientist and man of letters, who attended to the needs of his small flock 'mainly made of Scotchmen' from 1758-61. Priestley resided at Sweetbriar Hall, until he left Nantwich to take up a lectureship at the famous Dissenting Academy at Warrington, the nonconformist equivalent to the universities from which they were banned by the Test Acts. Though Priestley had hoped for the lectureship in science he was in fact appointed to a post in language and 'belles lettres'. However, his outstanding contribution to science was recognised when he was elected a Fellow of the Royal Society in 1776, largely for writings on the history of electricity, although he is more often remembered today for his discovery of oxygen.

Although Wesley preached at Bunbury and at Nantwich in the mid-18th century, the Nantwich circuit was only created in 1808, with 15 societies and 16 preachers. The old Baptist chapel in Barker Street was its first preaching house in Nantwich, but a large chapel was soon built in Hospital Street. The Primitive Methodists erected a chapel in Welsh Row in 1840, whilst other dissenters from Wesleyan practice built the Ebenezer chapel at Mill Street on the former site of the apprentice house of the cotton mill. Those of the Congregational persuasion had to wait until 1842, when a chapel was built opposite the Dysart Buildings in Churchyardside. The first Roman Catholic church was in St Anne's Lane, but the congregation moved to new premises in Pillory Street in the 20th century.

Nantwich lies near the junction of several canal systems leading to the West and to the Midlands. With the coming of the railways in the 1830s it was a natural site for a station of the Grand Junction Railway. However, such was the propaganda spread by the rival canal companies that the influential families of the area prevailed on the dignitaries of the town to reject the plans of the G.J.R. The canal companies in question were the Chester Canal Company and the Birmingham & Liverpool Junction Canal Company. The earliest canal to reach the basin outside the town on the Acton road was that from Chester, which had been approved by an Act of Parliament in 1772 and reached Nantwich in 1779. After a moderately prosperous few years, traffic fell off considerably and the company went into liquidation around 1790.

The Ellesmere canal through Shropshire to Llangollen was opened in part by 1795, though it was not completed through to Llangollen until the spectacular aqueduct at Pontcysyllte was completed in 1805. This canal was developed to allow access to the coal mines around Wrexham, but it was not an outstanding commercial success because the Trent & Mersey canal served much more industrialised areas in the Potteries and Midlands and provided access to Liverpool with its thriving trading association with America. Nantwich and Acton were also handicapped by this same waterway though they did have access to the Mersey at Ellesmere via the Chester canal.

Nantwich established two industries in the late 18th century, cotton spinning and boot and shoe manufacturing. Spinning was short lived since the main areas for this were in South Lancashire and North East Cheshire, but footwear manufacture continued until 1932. This industry originated in cottages, but eventually centred on small workshops and, from 1859, factories. Two long strikes in 1872 and 1873 led to the decline of the industry as factory masters found more amenable conditions in Midland towns. The basis of the trade had been the 'Nantwich boot' for workers in Lancashire and Yorkshire mills.

The workshops at Crewe were the main source of employment in the area, since the Directors of the L.N.W.R. actively discouraged the development of engineering at Nantwich, thus avoiding competition with their products. Men from Nantwich were nicknamed 'dabbers', a name said to be associated with the tanning industry in the town. Nantwich football club still carries this appellation.

As both towns expanded, factory masters recognised that the women of Nantwich and Crewe comprised an untapped pool of labour. The L.N.W.R. built a factory to manufacture uniforms in the vicinity of the works. This was opened by John Compton in 1865. A fustian factory was built by John Rigg in Henry Street in 1869 and let on lease to Mrs. Hall of Warmington. From these beginnings the clothing industry developed at both towns. The first purpose-built factory at Nantwich was opened on Barony Road in 1872 by Messrs. Harding & Co. of Manchester, though George Harlock had opened adapted premises in Welsh Row as early as 1855. Charles Doody & Sons manufactured ready-made clothes from the 1880s.

Crewe also tried to take over the cheese trade at Nantwich when a local railway contractor, John Hill, built the cheese market in 1845. Several cheese factors were attracted to Crewe, but the cheese fairs ceased in the 1870s. However, the L.N.W.R. initiated a market for cattle and horses, by transporting Irish animals on its line from Holyhead. The cattle auction in Gresty Road closed only recently, though the horse trade had declined by 1895. Today Nantwich is essentially an agricultural trading centre, whilst Crewe remains an engineering town. Both places have flourishing markets for local produce and goods from further afield.

The importance of the dairy industry to the economy of the county was recognised when the Dairy Institute was opened in an old farmhouse at Worleston in 1886. This was subsequently moved to form part of the Cheshire School of Agriculture at Reaseheath Hall near Nantwich. During the last war this was closed, but 1,200 volunteers for the Women's Land Army were trained on the premises. The school became a college in 1967. Since 1838, Nantwich has been the venue of one of the most important agricultural shows in the North-West, mounted in fields belonging to Dorfold Hall estate at Acton every July. The Cheese Fair at Nantwich is now the largest in Britain.

The urban development of Crewe began when the Grand Junction Railway was inaugurated in July 1837, linking the North-West with Birmingham via a junction at Warrington on the Liverpool-Manchester Railway. This was a crucial link in the railway system which was to lead to the western route between Scotland and London Euston. The company absorbed the Chester-Crewe Railway on 1 July 1840, and in turn both railways were amalgamated into the London and North Western Railway Company on 16 July 1846.

The Grand Junction Railway had built a small halt at Crewe on the Warrington-Birmingham line in 1837. By 1842 four lines radiated from this junction to Chester, Birmingham, Liverpool and Manchester. These were eventually joined by lines from Stoke-on-Trent (1848) and Shrewsbury (1858), the Stoke link being provided by the North Staffordshire Railway Company. The Great Western would have liked to gain a foothold on the west coast route but this was stoutly resisted by the L.N.W.R., though this company in turn was denied access to lines from Paddington to Birkenhead.

The town began to develop from 1843 onwards after Francis Trevithick, locomotive superintendent to the G.J.R., decided to move the engine workshop from Edge Hill, Liverpool, to Crewe. The area, known as Monk Coppenhall, was attractive to the directors of the G.J.R. because of its position, near the centre of the Midland Gap, and in the heavy claylands of central Cheshire so that large assembly shops could have firmly-based foundations. The land could also be bought inexpensively, being owned by Richard Edleston, a Nantwich lawyer who was favourably disposed to railway development. A workforce of 900 men, including engine builders, blacksmiths, millwrights and wheel-wrights, had to be accommodated beside the trackways leading to Crewe. The G.J.R. had no alternative but to provide housing and services for this large body of men and their dependents since they were to work in a sparsely-populated agricultural area of Cheshire.

The ancient town of Nantwich might have been a more logical choice since it lay at the hub of old established routeways, and town services had already been developed. Unfortunately the canal companies persuaded the old influential families that smoke emitted by the locomotives of the G.J.R. would be injurious to the health of people and livestock alike. For the same reason the town of Crewe grew up at some distance from the new railway station. In fact Crewe station was not within the town of Crewe until 1936, when the town boundary was extended into Church Coppenhall.

The town was built to a plan drawn up in 1840 by the G.J.R.'s Engineer-in-Chief, Joseph Locke. Two hundred and twenty-one houses were erected by 1843, and by 1851 a small town with a population of 4,491 existed, with 649 men gaining their livelihood in the L.N.W.R. works and sheds. Company housing stock was 441 by 1852. By 1900 the town had grown tenfold to accommodate a population of 43,237, with a railway workforce of 10,146 persons. Even by 1859 the growth of population was such that the railwaymen were able to raise the Volunteer Railway Corps in response to the threat of invasion of Great Britain by the French under Napoleon III.

The plans of the G.J.R. allowed for four classes of housing according to the status of employee. Senior management enjoyed large villas in their own grounds at Chester Street and middle management lived in Gothic-style houses. Skilled workmen were accommodated in detached villas, the so-called 'blockhouses', which housed four families, each with its own entrance and garden. Labourers lived in four-apartment terraced housing. The houses provided by the railway company were far superior to those provided for workers in other towns, and later by private speculation at Crewe. With the re-development of the town from the 1960s, most of the houses were demolished, but fortunately public protest preserved the few remaining properties in Dorfold Street, Betley Street and Lyon Street, which represent the terrace development. Works foremen were accommodated in terrace housing at Delamere and Victoria Streets, known locally as 'Gaffers Row'; some of these properties still exist. None of the managers' houses survived the redevelopment; such large properties were not suitable for private use.

The company piped in gas from its own plant on the southern boundary of the works and water was supplied from tanks, although senior management enjoyed a tapped supply. 'Night soil men' were employed to scavenge the streets and remove waste from the privies attached to each property. Unfortunately, both water supply and sewage disposal were effected via the Valley Brook! Since there was no provision for bathrooms in the workers' houses, the company provided public bathing facilities in 1845. These were under-used, since they were soon surrounded by the works' buildings, and were on wasteland which had no lighting provision. The replacement baths of 1862 were known locally as 'the porcelain baths' and contained a swimming pool. They were not replaced until 1937. It is reputed that the price of admission diminished as the water became dirtier during the course of the week. The company doctor looked after the health of the work-force, and a makeshift hospital was provided by adapting some cottages. Isolation hospitals were provided at a later date. The Cottage Hospital at Crewe dates from the early 20th century, a bequest by Francis Webb, chief mechanical engineer to the L.N.W.R., contributing greatly to its foundation. A company hospital to treat accidents in the works was built in Mill Street in 1911.

Whilst the L.N.W.R. provided most of the services required by the urban population of Crewe until the Act of Incorporation of 1877, the history of provision at Nantwich was very different. Early philanthropy was in the gift of religious houses or private individuals. A leper house, St Lawrence, was in existence at Acton in 1260. A hospice for the poor and travellers was established in Hospital Street, Nantwich, named after St Nicholas. Almshouses were provided both at Acton and at Nantwich. By the 19th century a work-house had been provided on The Barony; these buildings were incorporated into the Barony Hospital in the 1930s. The provision of services through local government was made possible by the Act of 1894. An Urban District Council looked after the town and its immediate environs, whilst villages in the old Hundred were the responsibility of the Rural District Council.

Such was the influence of the L.N.W.R. 'Crewe Committee' that even spiritual requirements were catered for. The former parish church was at Church Coppenhall, too remote for the new town centre. The company erected a small church in Moss Square which was to reach its final form only in 1906 when the north-east chapel was added. Most other Anglican churches of Crewe were provided by the company as the town expanded. All the Non-conformist denominations built chapels within the town, too. Only the huge former Congregational chapel at Hightown remains, now the Victoria Snooker Club.

Early educational endeavours started with the foundation of a grammar school at Nantwich in 1572, which opened in the disused Guildhall. Acton Grammar School was founded in 1662 but was closed in 1861, and in 1885 was added to the grammar school at Nantwich. The Delves of Doddington set up a charity school at Wybunbury in about 1820, under the terms of a bequest of 1746. Nantwich also had a bluecap school in Welsh Row. Possibly there was also an establishment at Crewe since a former public house was called *The Bluecap*.

The divisions of religion were also reflected in school provision at Crewe and, once again, it was the railway which supplied most educational premises at both elementary and technical level. The Church of England elementary school, Christ Church, provided education according to the 'national system' from the early days of the town. A larger Roman Catholic school was opened beside St Mary's church in 1879, whilst non-conformist education was provided by the Wesleyan school in Mill Street (1862) and the Presbyterian 'Scotch schools' (1869). A Presbyterian school for girls was opened in 1879 in Heath Street Hall. The much respected headmaster of the Scotch schools was William Wishart (1869-86) who undertook to train teachers through the pupil-teacher system.

With increasing public control of the town came the move to levy a rate for education, and to counteract this demand the L.N.W.R. was forced to increase its support for local schools. Ten further schools were built during the period 1866-1902, either wholly or partially financed by the company. No board schools were ever built in Crewe, though the Education Act of 1870 had allowed for the introduction of such a system. Church Coppenhall did set up a school board in 1873, which provided a National School in Broad Street and a smaller establishment at Maw Green.

The 1902 Education Act gave control of educational matters to borough or county councils and recognised the need to provide for separate secondary schools. The first council elementary school was opened in Brierley Street in 1908 at a cost of £20,000. It catered for 1,525 pupils, which in effect forced the now inadequate schools of the religious foundations to close their doors. All except St Mary's Catholic school did so. The lack of secondary schools in the town forced many parents to send their children to be privately educated. A few county scholarships were available at the ancient grammar schools at Nantwich and Sandbach, but these were totally inadequate to meet the needs of the expanding town. The county secondary school was designed by the county architect, H. Beswick, and opened in 1909 at Ruskin Road. The secondary education of girls remained a private venture of nuns of the Ursuline order, whose school had opened three years earlier in Nantwich Road. A further educational development was the opening of the teachers' training college, thanks largely to the efforts of Dr. W. Hodgson of Crewe, vice-chairman of the County Education Committee. Initially this was housed in the Mechanics' Institute, but from 1912 its base has been in purpose-built premises at Crewe Road.

The Mechanics' Institute was built in 1843 in Prince Albert Street, again by the L.N.W.R. and initially as a newspaper room for its employees. It had a controversial beginning when the company directors banned newspapers sympathetic to the Chartists' cause, with the result that most members withdrew their subscriptions. The L.N.W.R. then decided to construct a new building, complete with an assembly hall and classrooms for instruction in the '3 Rs' and mechanical drawing. This was opened in 1848-9 but again failed in its educational endeavours, being most often used for dancing, concerts and other public entertainment. But still the directors felt the Institute should fulfil an educational role. Technical instruction for workers commenced in 1855, when a prize system for apprentices was instituted. The 1869-71 building also housed the 'town hall', and a fitting and machine shop was installed. Further refinements were added over the years, for example a physics laboratory in 1903 and a chemistry laboratory in 1909. But the purpose of the Institute was always related closely to railway needs and the ultimate effect of this was to alienate the borough council. Thus a Municipal Technical Institute and School of Art was opened in Flagg Lane in 1897 and the Mechanics' Institute became purely a social club. The latter building was demolished in 1970, after standing derelict since 1966.

The leisure needs of the railwaymen and other inhabitants of Crewe were further satisfied when the Lyceum Theatre opened in 1887. The present building continues to serve the town as it has done since 1911. The local football club is one of the oldest in the Football League, having been founded in 1876 and admitted to the second division in 1892. Crewe Alexandra remained in this league for four years, then was out of the English League until election to the third division in the 1920-21 season. However, the club did have the satisfaction of winning the Welsh League cup in two consecutive years whilst out of English football. An outstanding figure in the club in the early 20th century was J. H. Pearson, who refereed the F.A. cup final and replay between Bradford City and Newcastle United in 1911. Others were Fred Keenor, who joined the club from Cardiff City in the mid-1930s, and Frank Blunstone and Johnny King who were transferred to higher status clubs at Chelsea and Stoke City respectively during the late 1950s.

The town's first library was donated by the L.N.W.R. in 1846, and in April 1936 the library and reading room of the Mechanics' Institute was converted into the public library. The present library is housed in the civic buildings of 1965, which are also the home of the police station and the county court. The civic buildings were erected over part of the site of 'Crewe Village', early housing erected by the G.J.R. and demolished at the start of the 1960s.

The red-brick Free Library at Nantwich dates from 1889, built by money raised by public subscription. This building was closed when the modern library in Beam Street was opened but in 1980 the old library was reopened as the Town Museum. The modern library was built on the site of the Technical Institute of 1902, since the South Cheshire College in Crewe provided more up to date facilities in 1966.

Public elementary education at Nantwich commenced when the Wesleyans opened a day school in 1840. The Marquis of Cholmondley provided the first National School in Nantwich a decade later. The Church of England schools in Market Street and Wood Street opened as a result of the Education Act of 1870. The schools at Market Street flourished until 1976, but that at Wood Street only had a short life.

The early local government of Crewe was vested in Monk Coppenhall Local Board which first met in 1860 in the Mechanics' Institute. The growth of the town led to petition for incorporation which was recognised in 1877. Nevertheless, railway interests were organised to protect the concerns of the L.N.W.R. The first mayor of Crewe was the company doctor James Atkinson who was of the Conservative persuasion. Several Chief Mechanical Engineers became mayors, the last being Bowen-Cooke. Even the last mayor of the old borough was a railwayman. Since so many services of the town, including most of the school provision, was in gift of the L.N.W.R., the company's 'Crewe Committee' was very jealous of its position. Matters came to a head in the mid-1880s, when it was revealed that workmen in the Crewe Works were being encouraged to look after the interests of L.N.W.R. nominees at local elections. Local papers were instrumental in many campaigns against the company monopoly. The 'intimidation affair' even reached the notice of Prime Minister W. E. Gladstone, who felt obliged to write a letter to the *Crewe Chronicle* deprecating the practice. The cost of not toeing the company line was loss of position in the works or, indeed, dismissal. Power even extended to foremen and senior charge hands in the works, and it was common practice to buy drinks for such men in local public houses. Presents were known to change hands in return for positions in the works.

Meanwhile, the railway employees were working to improve their original locomotive designs. During the decades up to the 1860s they perfected the original 2-2-2 design of George Stephenson, this standardisation of wheel arrangement providing a basis for company prosperity. By 1876, 2,000 steam locomotives had been built at the Crewe engine works; in 1911 the 5,000th engine, a 2-4-2 tank, had left the assembly line, an average of 75 locomotives per year from the inception of the G.J.R. works in 1843. From 1861 all locomotive building was centred on Crewe, so that it became the largest engine-building plant in the world. By the time the last steam locomotive left the works in 1958, a total of 7,357 had been built.

Many notable designs were drawn up by a succession of locomotive superintendents, the name given to the first engineers in charge and favoured up to the 1860s when the term 'chief mechanical engineer' came into vogue. These provided the motive power for local trains, goods haulage and main line passenger services including crack expresses. The early 2-2-2 design became obsolete and was replaced by ever more ingenious traction arrangements. An early success was the 0-6-0 locomotive designed for coal haulage, a development of an idea by John Ramsbottom, locomotive superintendent at the Longsight works near Manchester, and from 1861 the sole holder of this post with the L.N.W.R. Further modification of this design produced the engine known as the 'Newton'. From the 1870s express passenger trains were hauled by L.N.W.R. 'Precursors' and 'Precedents'. Compounding further increased the sophistication of the power generation system and was widely adopted by the company for both passenger loco-motives and those designed for freight trains. Thirty 'Experiments' were the first type of compound, being assembled from 1882 until 1884. Less powerful engines were based on a 2-4-0 tank design which was used for local trains and goods working. Perhaps the most magnificent looking locomotive was the giant eight-wheeled 'Webb compound' of 1893, named after Francis Webb, chief mechanical engineer from 1871 until 1903.

Larger engines were only designed after the retirement in 1891 of the autocratic chairman, Sir Richard Moon. The company was noted for the small size of its locomotives during his chairmanship. He insisted on such designs for economic running, which was further ensured by drivers being forbidden to run at a faster average speed than 39.5 m.p.h. However, Moon had to give way on the latter when the prestigious Royal Mail contract for the Holyhead line was successfully tendered for and an average running speed of 45 m.p.h. became necessary.

During the period 1904-7, 130 redesigned 'Precursors' came into service: these are described as 'simple, reliable and handsome locomotives' by the railway historian C. C. Dorman. The modification of the design was drawn up by George Whale, chief mechanical engineer 1903-9. The final L.N.W.R. design was the work of Captain H. P. M. Beames and hence was called the Beames 0-8-4T. This engine came into service in 1923, at which time the amalgamation of various companies led to the creation of the 'big four' railway companies which ran the network until post-war nationalisation brought about the formation of British Rail. The London and North Western Railway Company was taken over by the London, Midland and Scottish Company, which had for so many years been a close rival on the west coast route to Scotland. The L.M.S. had been formed at Derby. Altogether, 67 engine classes were built for the L.N.W.R. from 1846 to 1923, most of these at the Crewe works. The L.M.S. chief mechanical engineers in turn were to design some notable steam engines, but the story of the L.N.W.R. is so closely bound up with the development of Crewe that it seems fitting to conclude the locomotive story in 1923.

The Crewe works eventually expanded to cover 138 acres near the centre of the town. In the early days carriages had also been assembled here but the rationalisation when John Ramsbottom took over removed carriage building and that of other rolling stock to Longsight, Wolverton and Earlestown. The Deviation Works was built as part of the expansion programme (1866-8), and was so called because it stood beside the new deviation of the Chester line from Crewe. John Hill, chairman of the Monk Coppenhall Local Board, donated the land for the site of the steelworks, which began production in 1864. This works was an early user of the recently invented Bessemer process of steel manufacture. The Bessemer plant produced 1,000 tons of ingots per month during 1864-5. From 1874 the steelworks produced iron rails at a rate of almost 7,000 tons per annum, but after 1876 steel was used exclusively. Siemens' furnaces were also used at a later date. The steelworks closed in 1932, a victim of the many rationalisation programmes of the Depression.

The L.N.W.R. aimed to be completely self-sufficient in the products it needed. Though this was never entirely achieved, the company came very close. The workshops produced most of the fittings needed for locomotive manufacture in a wide variety of metals. From 1860, 1,000 steel tyres were manufactured each year. At one time there were 100 smithies in the works, 20 of which were solely concerned with the production of wheel centres. Springs were also produced for rolling stock. Reed lists some 50 products as having been manufactured at various times within the works complex. Perhaps the most bizarre were wooden legs. Two armoured trains for the defence of the east coast were built during the Great War and during both World Wars sections of the works were given over to the manufacture of gun parts and shells. No job seems to have been too small for the L.N.W.R. – it even made its own iron fencing to separate tracks from the surrounding countryside.

Any railway needs storage alongside its routeways, such as engine sheds, carriage sheds and warehousing. These were invariably built of brick in L.N.W.R. territory and such was the demand that the company found it more economic to have its own brickworks within the site complex rather than depend on outside producers. The first brickyard was in the vicinity of Eaton Street but a larger works was built off West Street in 1869. Amongst its products were the famous Crewe yellow bricks, which can still be seen in the walls of the Market Hall.

Crewe was, par excellence, the new town of the railway era. It was created wholly by the endeavours of the Grand Junction Railway and its successor, the London and North Western Railway Company, and it was once the proud boast of the latter that, 'Crewe is the L.N.W.R. and the L.N.W.R. is Crewe'. Perhaps the association is best remembered through the lovely Queen's Park developed on land donated by the directors of the L.N.W.R. to commemorate both the 50th anniversary of the foundation of the Grand Junction Railway and Queen Victoria's Diamond Jubilee. The railway workforce raised the subscription for the clock tower in the park.

However, the L.N.W.R. was not the only company to enjoy the railway facilities at Crewe. The North Staffordshire Railway operated an exchange siding off the main route to the north and opened a goods warehouse at Thomas Street in 1910. There is a tradition, probably unfounded, that the land for Queen's Park was donated to the town to prevent the Great Western Railway gaining extended services at Crewe. The G.W.R. was granted access to the south bays of the station in the 19th century and had its own booking office at the station. The company's locomotives were turned at Basford Hall, an extremely inconvenient arrangement necessitated by the denial of access to L.N.W.R. lines north of Crewe. The G.W.R. also had goods sidings in the marshalling yards. The yards at Gresty Road were very extensive, and there was even a post office there. The first post office opened in 1841 at the *Royal* Hotel near the station, and Crewe became a post town on 10 July 1846. The head post office opened with eight staff in 1855 and has since been based at various sites in the town. A large sorting office is still located near the station. Equally interesting was the vast traffic created by travelling post offices, 20 being routed through Crewe in the three hours after midnight in 1920.

Electrification of the main line was completed in 1961 and the station has been extensively remodelled over the past decade to take account of its new role. Crewe no longer serves a national freight market and the Gresty Road sidings have consequently been reduced, with the 'block train' system also contributing to their decline.

Crewe is no longer a one-company town, dependent exclusively on railway patronage. The first major impetus to alternative employment was the arrival of Rolls Royce Aero

Engines in 1938, the works being erected in record time as the war crisis deepened. At its peak the company employed 10,000 people, which did much to alleviate the stagnation in employment of the inter-war years. To attract the considerable investment required by the move of Rolls Royce, the corporation undertook to ensure that an adequate water supply was available, since the L.M.S. would only provide water after its own needs were satisfied. After the Second World War Rolls Royce based its automobile engineering division at Crewe and this remains the largest employer in the town today. The prestigious American company 'County Clothes' opened factories at Crewe in 1936 and 1938, and in the post-war period also took over some of the surplus capacity at the Rolls Royce Aero Engine plant, as did the Kelvinator Company until its move to Bromborough on the Mersey.

The final affirmation of the old borough of Crewe's corporate pride came when the Municipal Buildings were opened in Earle Street in 1905. The council never sought a grant of arms as did many other Cheshire boroughs in the 1930s, probably because of the economic difficulties in the town. The Crewe device consisted of a quartered shield depicting forms of transport from horse to canal, surmounted by a representation of a modern steam locomotive. Only in 1976 was this replaced by a genuine grant of arms celebrating the new borough of Crewe and Nantwich. The link with its neighbour in 1974 probably reflects a logical progression in administrative machinery to meet the needs of a larger community rather than a small industrialised town. The placing of the names has an historic precedent since Acton was subsumed with Nantwich from the 19th century, though Acton has been the ecclesiastical parish within which Nantwich was located in earlier days.

Although from the 1960s onwards the council has redeveloped much of the old town centre, giving a new face to Crewe, and consequently losing much heritage at a time when tourism is important to regional economy, the sense of civic pride still remains in a close-knit community of working people.

The new bypass through the old water meadows beside the River Weaver has relieved congestion in the historic town centre at Nantwich. This has been improved further by its designation as a pedestrian precinct. The people of the town are justifiably proud of the continuity of property that can be examined from the time of Queen Elizabeth I. The town preserves something of the feel of a medieval country town through its buildings, streetlines and narrow lanes.

Nantwich and Crewe complement each other and what other borough can proudly proclaim on entrances to the town that it is 'the home of the best car in the world'.

Buildings & Streets

1. Christ Church, Crewe. The tower, designed by J. W. Stansby, architect of the L.N.W.R., was added in 1877. It is surmounted by an iron crown, which was made in the Works.

2. Crewe Hall, from an old engraving. This house was built in the Jacobean style for Sir Ranulph Crewe in 1615-36. Although the son of a tanner in Hospital Street, Nantwich (see plate 25), Sir Ranulph became Lord Chief Justice during the reign of Charles I. His brother, Thomas, was Speaker of the House of Commons.

3. Originally a farmhouse, dating from 1639, this timber-framed building provides an interesting contrast with Crewe Hall. It became increasingly dilapidated in the 1920s when it was being used as a garage.

4. Hillock House, Hightown, Crewe. Despite its appearance, this house dates from the early 19th century: much of the 'timber' was painted-over brickwork. An earth tremor caused structural damage to its fabric, and Hillock House was demolished in 1926. Its site is now occupied by Jubilee Gardens.

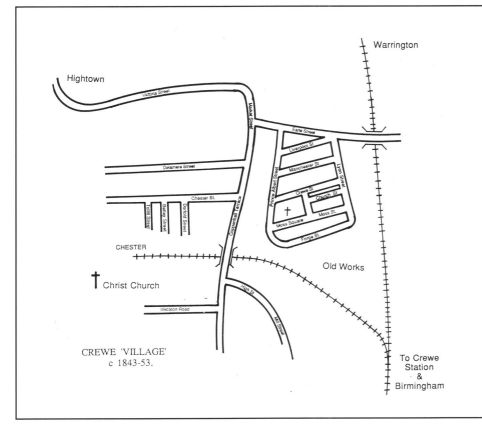

5. This plan shows the early street layout of Crewe 'village', as drawn by the chief engineer to the Grand Junction Railway, Joseph Locke. Houses for workmen were situated around Christ Church, and skilled craftsmen lived in nearby Prince Albert Street. Their accommodation was four apartment houses, known as 'blockhouses'.

6. The last remaining 'blockhouse' in Prince Albert Street. The decorative wooden bargeboard at the gable is a feature of housing in the 'village'. A wine bar is in the left-hand pair of houses, while the Railway Veterans Club, established by Bowen Cooke in 1919, occupies the right-hand pair.

7. In 1863 Chester Place was built as a residence for the Chief Mechanical Engineer of the L.N.W.R. with semi-detached homes for the Works Manager, Chief Draughtsman and other senior staff on either side. It is pictured *c.*1930, when H. P. M. Beames was still living there. He retired from the L.N.W.R. in 1922, but the L.M.S. allowed him to remain in Chester Place until he died, in 1934. The property was demolished in 1983.

8. 'Gaffers Row', Victoria Street, built 1854-6 to house the foremen of the L.N.W.R. They are similar to those in nearby Delamere Street and are a reminder that foremen and their families were segregated from workmen. In the 1980s, these properties were refurbished as bedsitters and flats.

9. The Grand Junction Railway insisted that an open space, now the Market Square, was left in the centre of Crewe when the town was planned, at Coppenhall Terrace. During the 19th century the L.N.W.R. allowed a market here, and from 1883 the main post office was located in the market square. Until its demolition in 1983, the Odeon was here too, the last of three cinemas. In the 1950s the square was remodelled, and on 2 November 1955 Her Majesty the Queen opened the development and named it Queensway. Since this date a modern shopping precinct has been built behind Market Street.

10. Crewe's Market Hall, photographed here in 1920, was built by John Hill, the railway contractor for the L.N.W.R. in 1845. This attempt to attract cheese fairs away from Nantwich failed two decades after the first Crewe fair of 1849. Note the Cheese Hall Hotel with its splendid lamp.

11. The Municipal Buildings in Crewe stand on Earle Street (named after one of the early directors of the G.J.R. and its successor, the L.N.W.R.). Built in 1902-5 to the English Baroque design of H. J. Hare, a striking feature is the façade, shown here. The allegorical figures represent the industries of Crewe. Marble of many different colours decorates the fine entrance hall.

12. Church Street, Crewe, looking west towards Christ Church. This was built by the G.J.R. because Coppenhall St Michael, the parish church, was too far from Crewe 'village'.

13. Church Street, Crewe, looking east towards Lyon Street. A tower of the Old Works is visible at the end of the terrace. The wall on the east side of Lyon Street marks the west boundary of the Old Works.

14. Manchester Street, Crewe. The corner shop is a ubiquitous feature of every Victorian industrial town. Each pair of houses is served by two front doors on every porch.

15. This display of kitchen equipment advertises 'Kitchen Corner', Hightown, Crewe. The electric washing machine still has a hand wringer, while water was heated by a gas boiler on the wall. Beside the gas cooker is a meat safe, where meat could be stored away from flies. Equipment dates from 1950.

16. As Crewe borough grew, Church Coppenhall and then more peripheral areas towards the Middlewich road and along the main road from Crewe to Nantwich became popular residential suburbs away from the grime of the old town. This advertisement, c.1930, emphasises the healthy environment and low purchase price on this estate, situated near the Crewe to Nantwich road.

17. Victoria Street, Crewe, *c*.1930. Although an important shopping area with shops located on the north side, opposite 'Gaffers Row', the small amount of motor traffic could be controlled easily by the policeman on point duty. The Victoria Centre has now been built nearby.

18. St Mary's Church, Nantwich. A chapel was first recorded on this site in 1130, but the present building dates mainly from the 14th century: the lierne vaulted chancel, for example, was built in 1380. A noteworthy church treasure is the only copy in England of the *Sarum Hymns and Sequences*, of 1502. This is a book of hymns and orders of divine service associated with Salisbury Cathedral.

19. Interior of St Mary's, from an illustration in James Hall's *History of the Town and Parish of Nantwich* (late 19th century). The stone pulpit is 15th century, while this print shows clearly the fine decoration over the crossing arch, and the board bearing the Ten Commandments.

20. The Congregationalist Chapel, Nantwich, was erected in 1842 at Churchyardside. Sunday school provision in an adjoining building followed. These properties were redeveloped as housing after they were made redundant, following reorganisation of non-conformist churches.

21. Preacher's House, Hospital Street, Nantwich. When the Central Methodist chapel was erected in 1808 two houses for preachers were provided. The Primitive Methodist chapel in Welsh Row followed in 1840, on the site of an old cloth merchants' hall given by George Wilbraham.

22. This picture shows the properties on the north side of Hospital Street. Recent archaeological excavations have shown that in Tudor times there were only scattered houses here, which faced towards marshland on the south side of the road. On the extreme left is Sweetbriar Hall.

23. Sweetbriar Hall, the timber-framed house of the Wilbrahams of Woodhey was built in the 15th century, and the octagonal bay window was added in the 16th century. This engraving shows the interesting window lights of the original hall. During the 18th century the timber work was covered by plaster. Sir James Bowman, the notable Victorian surgeon, was born here.

24. The Rookery, Hospital Street. A Georgian façade covers the original Tudor timber frame, disguising the fact that this house once had a central hall flanked by wings, in the style of Churche's Mansion or 116 and 140 Hospital Street. Only Churche's Mansion remains as designed, while the other three were altered to conform with 18th-century fashion.

25. The jettying on the front of 140 Hospital Street betrays the building's Tudor origins, otherwise well hidden by rendering. Reputed to stand on the site of St Nicholas' Hospital, it was occupied by John Crewe, father of Sir Ranulph, in the 17th century.

26. These Elizabethan cottages in Welsh Row, Nantwich, have now been converted into one dwelling, known as 'Malthouse Cottage', which commemorates an earlier use of the building.

27. Wattle and daub, in the *Crown Hotel*, Nantwich (see plate 93). Plaster has been removed to show the wattles of hazel and willow. The daub that covered this consisted of, for example, ox blood, horsehair and animal dung. This building dates from 1584.

28.   In 1629 this Elizabethan building, White Hall, Nantwich, was occupied by the Wettenhall family. Adam de Wettenhall was sent to Ireland on the king's business in 1276. Another Wettenhall, Henry, was in the bodyguard of Richard II. The rear of the house, seen here, faced on to Welsh Row; there were extensive views at the front. An antiques business founded here in 1892 continued until the early 1950s, and the Hall was demolished in 1970. This photograph was taken c.1930.

29.   Welsh Row, Nantwich. A fine Tudor house is adjacent to the Georgian Townwell House, so-named as a town well was nearby. The jettying, so typical of Tudor buildings, was used to evade fire regulations which specified a minimum distance between dwellings – but only at street level. Before the mid-19th century, Welsh Row was known as le Frog Row, this being a local name for the open channel sewer which ran along the centre of the street.

30. The largest open space in Nantwich town centre, the High Street, is pictured here in 1868. Robert Dixon owned a grocery shop here, which was later taken over and became Zan Stores. Carringtons Newsagency also occupied a site here in the triangle of buildings between Swine Market and Oat Market.

31. Churche's Mansion, Nantwich, is one of the finest examples of Cheshire timber and stucco work. Timber has been stripped of its black paint to reveal the natural colour of the wood. Ornamentation on the first floor is different from that on the ground floor and gables. Many original interior features have been retained, including beautiful panelling.

32. Often one needs to look above ground floor level to appreciate the true age of buildings. 46-48 High Street, Nantwich, are Tudor and provided two homes in the 16th century. Thomas Church, a mercer, and nephew of Richard Church who built Churche's Mansion, had his shop and home at number 46, while Thomas's nephew, William, lived next door.

33. The elaborately-decorated gable shown here overlooks Castle Street and is a detail of 46-48 High Street, shown above. The timber brackets that support the jetty are all carved.

34. Queen Elizabeth donated money towards the rebuilding of this house in Nantwich, hence its name: Queen's Aid House. The inscription on the façade, shown in plate 35, records her generosity towards the town. Built in 1584, and photographed here *c*.1924, the house remains a good example of Tudor architecture, despite modification of the windows during the 19th century.

35. The decoration of Queen's Aid House illustrates the superb craftsmanship of Thomas Cleese, a carpenter who was much involved with rebuilding property after the Great Fire.

36. On a corner site opposite the Swine Market in Nantwich stands a very fine late 16th-century jettied building. Number 16 High Street may not have original windows but they are faithful replicas, and the later Georgian windows are not too intrusive.

37. In this view of Pillory Street, Nantwich, taken in 1905, the Victoria Cocoa House is shown on the right, while the tree opposite stands at the entrance to the Quaker burial ground and meeting house. The Cocoa House was rebuilt and renamed to commemorate Victoria's Diamond Jubilee, and provided a meeting place for those, such as Quakers, who preferred not to patronise licensed premises.

38. Old Gaol House, also in Pillory Street, has now been replaced by the town museum. It is a good example of the smaller houses in Nantwich at the time of the Great Fire, which was eventually checked near this house.

39. In Tudor days the pillory, a replica of which is located opposite the museum, was used to punish bakers found guilty of malpractice. This was not the only public humiliation: a ducking stool was to be found at Cartlake, near Wall Lane. It was a punishment for women who were accused of being scolds or witches.

40. This notice is attached to the gable end of a house in South Crofts in Nantwich, acting as a reminder that many roads were private and maintained by householders. South and North Crofts commemorate the former lands of Combermere Abbey in the town; the monastery was dissolved by order of Henry VIII in 1539.

NOTICE
This is a private road.
It is not a CART ROAD or a HORSE ROAD
All Persons offending will be
PROSECUTED.
BY ORDER.
This will be strictly enforced.

Industry & Agriculture

41. In 1878 the capabilities of Crewe Works were demonstrated when this locomotive was built in 25½ hours.
These '17 inch coal engines' were the cheapest ever produced at Crewe, costing only £500 each. Though small compared
with engines of rival companies they were capable of very hard work, and considerable standardisation of parts made them
easy to repair.

42. The only Locomotive Superintendent of the L.N.W.R. from 1861, when McConnell (superintendent of the Southern Division) retired, was John Ramsbottom. He reorganised the company to divide resources and products more efficiently, and Crewe became the locomotive building centre. Ramsbottom's most famous design was the 0-6-0 DX engine (plate 74) of which 943 were built. It was the first 'mass-produced' design from the works.

43. By 1880, when this photograph was taken, the works had expanded to over 100 acres, with many lines connecting workshops and mills. Small shunting engines were designed by Webb for works use only.

44. Perhaps the most inventive of any of the Chief Mechanical Engineers of the L.N.W.R. was Francis Webb. He was a strong-willed man who served the railway well and was influential in Crewe, making generous provision for the town both during his lifetime and in his will. Webb was mayor from 1886-7 and was given the freedom of Crewe in 1903.

45. George Whale succeeded Webb as C.M.E. in 1903, holding the office until 1909. Like Webb he was a Premium apprentice, entering Wolverton Works, but transferring to Crewe as a locomotive draughtsman in 1865 when his apprenticeship ended. Whale too was mayor of Crewe, from 1885-6.

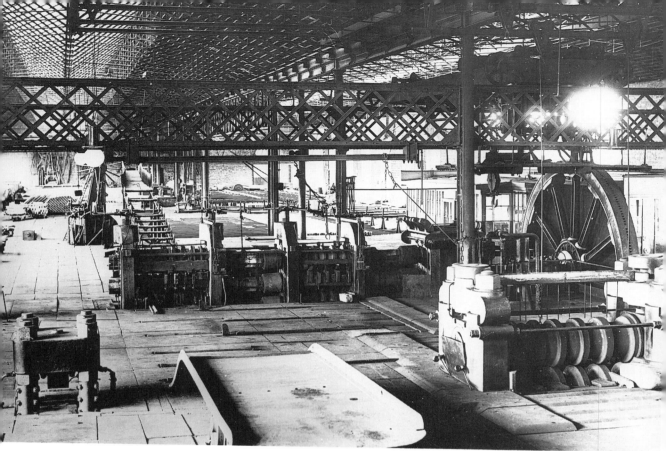

46. This view shows the rail and cogging mills in 1891, by which time the Works was almost self-sufficient. From 1874 steel rails were produced, as the price of steel had become competitive with iron. Originally the steel works concentrated on locomotive parts.

47. In the 19th century the L.N.W.R. acquired the Shropshire Union Railway and Canal Company. One of the more unusual products of Crewe Works was this canal barge, constructed entirely of steel. It was a day barge only, used for maintenance work: the aft cabin was a mess room, the fore cabin for tools.

48. By 1906 much of the machinery in the fitting shop dated from the Ramsbottom era, and a few machines still carried the insignia of the Grand Junction Railway!

49.   Crewe Works, 1909, viewed from the south. The steelworks end of the complex is shown. To the left there is the rivetting tower of the boiler shops and a wooden cooling tower; in the centre the chimneys of the carriage works and melting furnaces; on the right the three chimneys of the steel foundry.

50.   The shunters (seen here in 1911) played an important role in the handling of freight in Crewe's goods yards. Coupling and uncoupling wagons, often while trains were moving, called for fine judgement and skilled use of the shunter's pole: any slip could result in death or mutilation.

51. By 1914, when this photograph was taken, about ninety locomotives were being built in Crewe Works per year, while about the same number were scrapped, and over 1,000 were under repair. Among the assembly crew shown here is Henry Lindop's father: three generations of the family worked at Crewe.

52. General Offices, Crewe Works, 1915. Built beside the old Chester line in 1876, they housed the design centre, together with offices for senior management.

53. Mr. and Mrs. Edward Joinson of Coppenhall, Crewe. Teddy Joinson was a Master Painter in the Works, where all decoration on the locomotives was hand-painted. Their house in Reid Street still stands, complete with the iron gate that was spared when metal was collected during the Second World War. This was because Teddy, blind in later life, used to lean over the gate to talk to passers-by.

54. Bowen-Cooke succeeded Whale as Chief Mechanical Engineer, and held the post for 11 years, serving the L.N.W.R. well during the First World War. A notable design of this era was the 4-6-2 tank engine series, but Cooke also designed several freight locomotives, based on modifications of the 0-8-0 design of Francis Webb.

55. Rolls Royce Motor Cars Ltd. moved to Crewe from Derby in 1946. This photograph shows the Derby factory in the 1930s.

56.   The aero engine division of Rolls Royce had moved to Crewe before the Second World War. The first test bays were erected at Pym's Lane in 1939.

57.   The Rolls Royce Merlin engine, being assembled here in 1940, was used to power Spitfires and Hurricanes, the Lancaster bomber (in a modified form) and the Mosquito night fighter.

58.   At 3.09pm on Sunday 29 December 1940, a Junkers 88 bombed the Rolls Royce works, causing extensive damage. Sixteen workers were killed.

59.   County Clothes was an American company that opened in Crewe before the war. They made uniforms for American officers stationed in Britain, thus saving valuable space on Atlantic convoys. This photograph appeared in a newspaper with the caption '... somewhere in England'.

60. When war ended in 1945, the Rolls Royce aero division moved back to Derby, where the research department was located. At this stage the motor car division moved to the vacated premises, so the highly skilled workforce at Crewe was not wasted. This photograph shows the polishing shop in 1946.

61. Many companies set up works fire units to tackle fires before the municipal brigade arrived. The volunteer brigade at Rolls Royce, seen here in 1949, obviously could operate only on a limited scale.

62. The Rolls Royce trim shop, 1955.
Only the finest quality hides are used
to cover the seats of Rolls Royce cars,
and as they are so expensive the craft
of cutter is highly skilled. On the right
of the picture, machinists are
assembling panels for the seat covers.

63. During the Second World War women were recruited for the first time at Rolls Royce. At first they were so resented that the men went on strike for a week, but soon women were accepted and became skilled workers, such as the capstan lathe operators, pictured here in 1967.

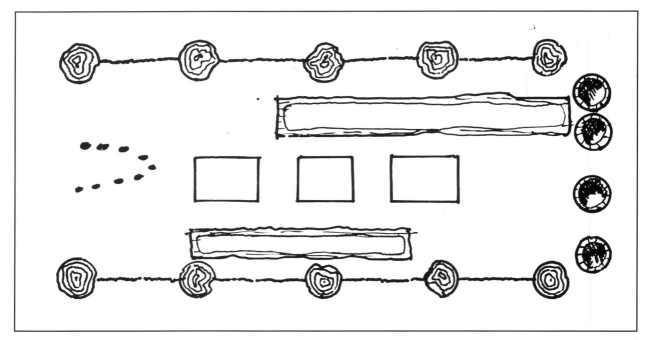

64. A plan of the medieval salthouse in Wood Street, Nantwich. It had 12 pans, was 10-12m. long and 8m. wide. The barrels sunk into the ground may have been used to clean tools, brine being very corrosive. Two hollowed out tree trunks (ships) were used to store brine, which was evaporated in lead pans over a wood fire (centre). Wood to fuel the fires was kept on the site of Wood Street, hence its name.

65. This reconstruction of the salthouse shows the salt rakes and wicker baskets. New salt was probably stored in the baskets so any remaining liquid could drain away. The thatched roof is conjectural.

66. The brine spring named Old Biot was the source of Nantwich's early prosperity: salt ('wych') is mentioned in Domesday Book. It still bubbles up in the banks of the River Weaver to the east of Nantwich bridge.

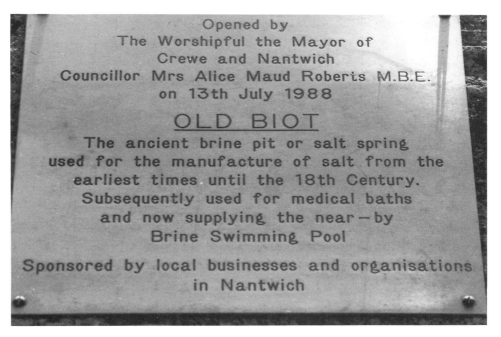

Opened by
The Worshipful the Mayor of
Crewe and Nantwich
Councillor Mrs Alice Maud Roberts M.B.E.
on 13th July 1988

OLD BIOT

The ancient brine pit or salt spring
used for the manufacture of salt from the
earliest times until the 18th Century.
Subsequently used for medical baths
and now supplying the near–by
Brine Swimming Pool

Sponsored by local businesses and organisations
in Nantwich

67. A typical scene at harvest time in the countryside around Crewe and Nantwich at the turn of the 19th century, as farmworkers take a rest from heavy labour. Children have brought them refreshments, including a billy can of tea and a stone jar of small beer.

68. Until enclosure in 1838, Ravensmoor, Burland by Acton, was common land. The windmill pictured here was adapted to pump water before 1891 when 'Liverpool water' was supplied to the area.

69. The Old Mill, Volunteer Fields, Nantwich, is a fine
19th-century building which was possibly once a boot and
shoe manufactory. The street name commemorates the
Volunteers who may have drilled on this part of Beam Heath.

70. In 1938 the sole-surviving cotton spinner in Nantwich
was Mrs. Sarah Wainwright. A cotton mill had been opened
in 1789 by Thomas Bower, on a site beside the River Weaver.
It became a corn mill in 1874, as the company could no longer
compete with the centralised spinning mills of north-east
Cheshire and Lancashire.

71. Millstone Lane, Nantwich, contains typical examples of late 19th-century artisan housing. These cottages are known locally as Tanners Row because Harvey's Tannery was sited behind them.

72. The Chester canal reached Nantwich in 1779, and warehouses were soon built around the basin. The cheese warehouse shown here was used by cheese factors (wholesalers), who stored cheeses here before resale to the retail trade. The arrangement of doors and evidence of hoists indicate that produce could be transferred directly from canal to road.

Transport

73.   The first station at Crewe was built in 1837, and was a small halt. It soon became obvious that this was inadequate for a main line and in 1845-6, when this engraving was made, a larger station was built. A canopy was added in 1848.

75. Crewe Works produced a wide range of products, including trackside equipment such as this mileage post. This was made at the Deviation Works which stood beside the Chester line from Crewe.

LONDON & NORTH WESTERN RLY
NOTICE.
IT IS FORBIDDEN FOR VAGRANTS, BEGGARS, ITINERANT MUSICIANS AND FEMALES OF DOUBTFUL REPUTATION TO ENTER THESE PREMISES.

MAY 1901   BY ORDER

76. Another example of the smaller trackside fittings which were made at Crewe Works.

74. Crewe Junction, viewed from the south-east, in 1866. The engines are Trevithick/Allan designs (in production until the 1870s) except for the central locomotive in the right hand row: an 0-6-0 DX designed by Ramsbottom. Trevithick was the first Locomotive Superintendent of L.N.W.R. and Allan was his Works Foreman, the equivalent of the later Works Manager. Some signals are of the old slotted post type.

London & North Western Railway.

In your reply give this Reference

Reference to your Letter.

Locomotive Department.

Crewe Station.

June 8th 1875

Dear Sir

June 9

I am arranging for our Wesleyan School Trip to Rhyl Llandudno & Bangor on the 7th July. Will you please exhibit bills & sell tickets for us as before? The train will start from at your Station.

Yours Truly

W. M. Lambert

77. In 1875 the station-master at Nantwich received this letter, concerning an excursion train, from Crewe Works. The train was to depart from Nantwich Junction and run to Crewe, where it would join the main line to Chester and North Wales.

78. Lord Crewe's private siding at Crewe Station, pictured here in 1881, contains wagons belonging to the Madeley Coal and Iron Company. The *Crewe Arms*, where once Queen Victoria dined, was built by the L.N.W.R. and is still one of the town's premier hotels. Beside the platform there stand three travelling post office coaches, a horse box and two closed wagons.

79. Production of the Webb 'Compound' Teutonic class ended in 1903, but this example, 'Jeanie Deans', remained in service until 1906. From 1891-9 she hauled the prestigious Euston-Crewe express, and was noted as an economical runner.

80. At the turn of the century the L.N.W.R.'s General Manager became worried that the company's reputation for punctuality was being lost. In 1901 double-headed trains were introduced to increase average speeds. Shown here is a Precedent-class 2-4-0 locomotive, the first of which was built in 1874, piloting a Webb compound at the head of a train of new-style eight wheel carriages.

81. Until the 1970s Crewe was an important freight-handling centre. After this date national freight movement has concentrated at Warrington and Crewe is now only locally significant. This picture shows a coal train at Crewe South, c.1910, being worked by a Webb goods engine.

82. Crewe North signal box, 1906. By this time signals were being operated by electricity. The Chester line branches to the left, the Glasgow-London line to the right. In the middle of the picture is the Old Works, while the Crewe Alexandra Football Club stand, at Gresty Road, is in the background.

83. Bowen Cooke designed this tank engine class. No. 1006 was in service from 1912 to 1936. Tank engines were so-named because water was stored in tanks before it was introduced into the boiler, thus eliminating the need for a large tender.

84. Sir Gilbert Claughton (1856-1921) was chairman of the L.N.W.R. from 1911 to 1921. The Claughton class locomotives, an example shown here passing Minshull Vernon, north of Crewe, en route to Euston in 1913, were named after him.

85. This photograph illustrates another locomotive class, at Oxenholme in 1916. 'Ramillies' was built in the Webb era, but modified by Whale. She remained in service from 1900 to 1930. The branch line to Windermere is on the left, and the Caledonian Railway coach and newspaper van are also worthy of note.

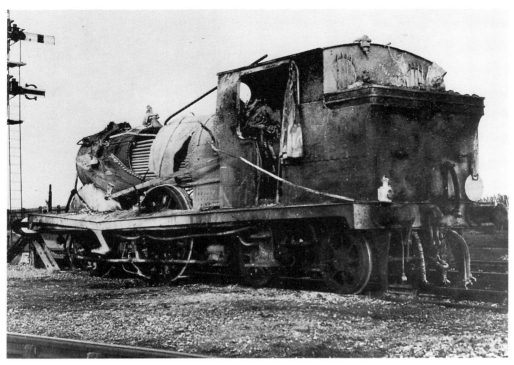

86. Few details are known about this accident. The locomotive frame has been severely distorted in a head-on collision and the double skin of the boiler has been ripped open to reveal the fire tubes.

87. This depressing sight is of four locomotives awaiting the 'scrapman's torch' in 1936 at Crewe Works.

88.   Electrification of the Crewe to Manchester line in 1958 was the beginning of the end for steam haulage. Much civil engineering work was involved in the changeover to electricity, including the raising of bridges.

89.   The last steam locomotive was built at Crewe Works in 1958, and the final repair was completed in 1967. Main-line diesel engines entered service in 1959, diesel shunters a year earlier. This locomotive is named after Sir Brian Robertson, the chairman of the British Transport Commission from 1953 to 1961.

90. Hurstfield Travel began as a shipping agent as this advertisement of *c.*1930 indicates. The service conveyed goods by rail to the point of embarkation; tourism was a logical development.

91. Samuel Jackson and Sons Ltd. began as builders of road-mending equipment, later diversifying into agricultural machinery. Their premises were at the junction of the Crewe to Nantwich road with that to Willaston, known as Jackson's Corner.

92.   In 1552 William Chatterton, Groom in Ordinary to Queen Mary, was granted a licence to keep a tavern in Hospital Street, Nantwich. The *Lamb Hotel* became one of the town's coaching inns, and the archway under the lamp gave access to the stables. The first firehouse in Nantwich, which dates from 1746, was located nearby.

93.   *Crown Hotel*, Nantwich, *c.*1910. This inn was formerly known as the *Crown and Sceptre* and was a famous coaching inn on the Chester to London road. Crown Mews, beside the inn, was the entrance to the stables at the rear of the property.

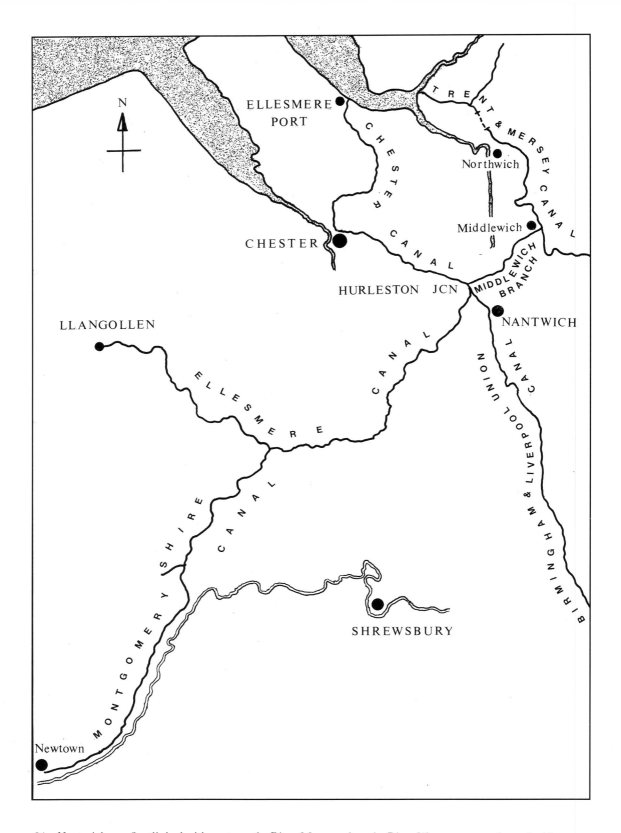

94. Nantwich was first linked with ports on the River Mersey when the River Weaver was made navigable up to the town in 1734, to ease the transportation of salt. The canal, linking Nantwich with Chester and the Mersey, has already been mentioned. Today the canal basin is a marina and centre for boat hire.

95. Nantwich Aqueduct was built to the design of Thomas Telford, and carries the canal over the Acton Road. It allows barges to travel west into the Shropshire Union Canal and thence to Wales.

96. The stables at Bunbury shown here were required by horses that pulled fast flyboats along the Shropshire Union Canal. As in the days of stagecoaches, 'express' services regularly needed fresh horses. The 80-mile journey from the Mersey ports to the Black Country could be completed in 24 hours.

97. The canal company had a warehouse and offices at Bunbury, illustrated here, and there was also a staircase of locks. The Shropshire Union Company foresaw future involvement with railways, but the plan was abandoned when the L.N.W.R. took over the canal lease in 1849.

98. On the outskirts of Wrenbury there are several lift bridges of which this is one example. It is unique since it allows a road to cross the canal. Nearby a former mill is occupied by English County Cruisers, and towards the village an old cornmill has been refurbished and is now an inn and restaurant.

99. In 1827 a branch from the Shropshire Union Canal at Barbridge Junction to the Trent and Mersey Canal, via Middlewich, was opened. This connected both Nantwich and Acton with the Midlands and the port of Liverpool. In spite of this they did not gain much from canal traffic, and railways soon eclipsed even this development.

100. In the autumn of 1942 a culvert collapsed at Shebdon, Staffordshire, closing the canal for many months while repairs were carried out. In many places the opportunity was taken to drain sections for maintenance, and the photograph shows this happening to the south of Nantwich basin. The V-shaped canal section is very obvious.

101. Maintenance work near Acton. Dredging of canals has to take place regularly to prevent them from silting up. The bucket dredgers are dumping the excavated sediment into a disused barge.

102. The branchline from Nantwich to Market Drayton was opened by the G.W.R. in 1863. Mr. Dunton, to whom the memorandum, dated 1868, is addressed, was presumably the Nantwich station-master.

GREAT WESTERN RAILWAY. February 25th 1868
(45)
MEMORANDUM.—From MARKET DRAYTON to Nantwich

C5745

G. N. Rope "JJ"

Dear Sir,

The above entered Audlem to Grantham August 27th sent you in Break van same day for transfer, please trace forward (said not to hand) and prove delivery, I believe you sent the above on to Stafford.

Mr Dunton. Stafford 26th

Yours truly
J. P. Collett
Attes.

103. Nantwich Junction, shown here, was called 'junction' because the G.W.R. line from Market Drayton joined the L.N.W.R. line to Shrewsbury here. In the late 19th century thousands of gallons of milk were dispatched each week from the station to supply Lancashire towns.

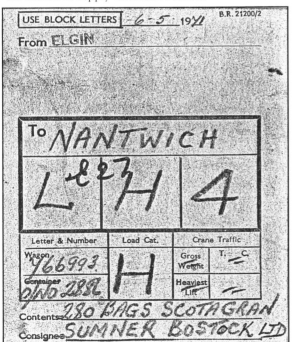

104. This railway dispatch note suggests that the efficiency of freight handling has improved since the 19th century. Elgin lies in a fertile grain-growing area of eastern Scotland. Shortly after this date, Nantwich station was closed to freight traffic as part of the rationalisation programme initiated by Dr. Beeching, Chairman of the British Railway Board, 1963-7.

MOTOR TRANSPORT

OF GOODS TO AND FROM

**LIVERPOOL,
BIRKENHEAD,
MANCHESTER,
WARRINGTON, Etc.**

Estimates given for large or small consignments.

TELEPHONE 5490.

P. NORTH,

CREWE ROAD END, **NANTWICH.**

105. When this advertisement appeared, c.1930, bulk transportation of goods by road was beginning to compete with railways. This firm had obviously built up a lucrative business with towns along the Mersey.

Charities & Education

106.   Francis Webb left £70,000 in his will to establish an orphanage in Victoria Avenue, Crewe, for children of railway employees. It was built in 1909 and is presently used as a staff training centre for British Rail Engineering Ltd.

107.   Pedley Street Elementary School, Crewe, was built in 1897 by the L.N.W.R. for £3,500. It was almost the last school to be provided by the company. The street is named after Richard Pedley (1828-1909) of Haslington, who was the first cheese factor to set up business in Crewe.

108. Dissatisfied with the quality of technical instruction of the Mechanics' Institute founded by the L.N.W.R. in 1846, the Education Committee sanctioned the building of a Technical Institute. This opened in Flag Lane in 1897, a government tax on whisky having provided its funding! The Borough Council met here until the Municipal Buildings were opened in 1905.

109. This pleasing terracotta panel is an example of the decoration on the exterior of the Institute. Other buildings in Crewe of the same style display similar ornamentation.

110. The first training college for teachers was established in the Mechanics' Institute in 1908, but it moved to purpose-built accommodation, illustrated here, in 1912. The college has since amalgamated with the institution at Alsager, to form the Crewe and Alsager College of Higher Education.

111. Ruskin Road School, Crewe, was designed by H. Beswick, the county architect, and opened in 1909. It was a grammar school for boys. D. H. McCurtain was the first headmaster, from 1909 to 1938.

112. Crewe Council provided Ludford Street secondary school in 1931. It offered a more technical and commercial curriculum than the grammar schools, and thus prepared many pupils for employment on the railway. The objectives of the school are engraved on the façade. Part of the premises is now used as Crewe Reading Centre.

113. Charity in the area did not begin with the provision of education by the L.N.W.R. Roger Wilbraham of Dorfold Hall built these almshouses in Acton churchyard in 1613, and also four others for men of Nantwich at Welsh Row. They are good examples of 17th-century estate cottage architecture.

114. The Crewe almshouses in Beam Street, Nantwich, were provided in 1767 by the joint philanthropy of Sir Thomas and Sir John Crewe, the executor of their wills being John Crewe. They stand on the site of a Wilbraham family town house which had been demolished to make way for a House of Correction and Workhouse in the late 17th century. Seven poor men were housed, each having a garden and £6 per year.

115. In 1638, Sir Edmund Wright provided Wright's almshouses – originally sited on part of the lands of
St Nicholas' Hospital, but now re-erected alongside the Crewe and Hope Almshouses in Beam Street. This
development was re-opened by Princess Alexandra. Wright was a native of Nantwich, but he had made his
fortune in London, being its Lord Mayor in 1640-1.

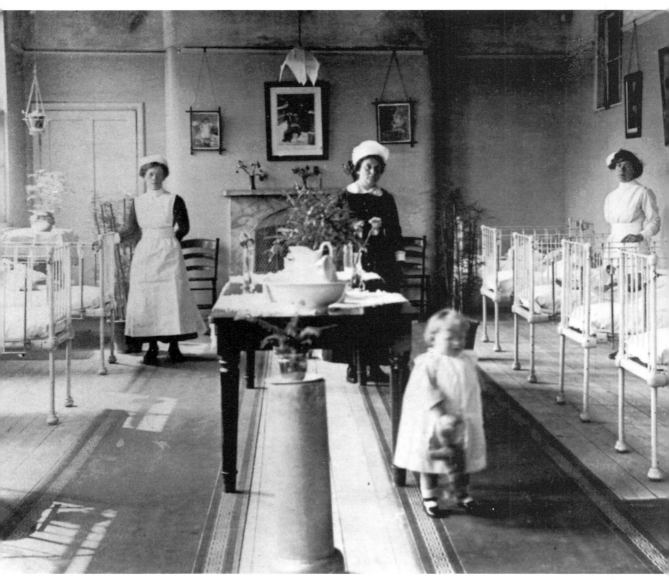

116. A house of correction and workhouse stood in Hospital Street, Nantwich, in the 17th century. Two centuries later
the workhouse pictured here *c.*1920 was built for the Nantwich and Acton Union. This is the children's dormitory, and
although the cots are regimented, the room has been brightened with pictures and flowers.

117. Tollemache Almshouses, Welsh Row, Nantwich, were built in 1870 to replace the 17th-century Wilbraham almshouses. They are said to be on the site of the Hospital of St Lawrence, a leper house of 1260. The Tollemache family was related to the Earl of Dysart (after whom the Dysart Buildings in Churchyardside are named) and its coat of arms is visible over the middle cottage's doorway.

118. The rights and privileges of the Beam Heath trustees originated in Saxon times and they were appointed by Act of Parliament. Beam Heath Estate, comprising Willow Farm, the Ley and other lands around Nantwich, was administered by this group, pictured here in 1919.

119. Delves Charity School, Wybunbury, educated 20 boys and 10 girls when it opened *c.*1820. This is indicated by the following, which is dated 4 May 1746:

> Rents and profits ... to buy blue coats and caps for poor (children) who have no relief from the Overseers of the said parish at a rate of
>> 10 shillings per cap and coat   £10
>> blue gowns and bonnets   £5
> To be bought against Easter every year.

120. Nantwich Grammar School was founded in 1572, at the expense of John and Thomas Thrush of London, woolpackers and natives of Nantwich. It was established in this building, the Guildhall, in St Mary's churchyard. The master was required to be a Church of England clergyman, and to be licensed to teach by the bishop of Chester. Charity commissioners visited in 1836, and reported on the poor buildings and inadequate endowment. The first non-clerical schoolmaster was appointed only in 1831.

121. The Wesleyans provided the first elementary schooling in Nantwich from 1840. Their earliest school was destroyed by fire in 1908 and these premises, in Hospital Street, replaced it. In 1911, however, this school was itself superseded by the Manor Road Council Schools.

122. The first school provided by the Church of England in Nantwich was a Sunday school, built in 1837 on land in Market Street given by John Tollemache. In 1876 the first day school was established, on the same site, and this closed in 1974. Pupils are pictured here in 1913, when the curriculum included Swedish drill, music and creative activities.

123.　Worleston Dairy Institute was opened in an old farmhouse in 1886, aiming to improve farmhouse cheese production. Students and staff are shown here in 1914. When the institute closed in 1926 students were transferred to the School of Agriculture at Reaseheath Hall, and the building reverted to its original use, as Aston Hall Farm. It is located on the Worleston to Aston-juxta-Mondrum road.

124. Cheshire County Council had purchased Reaseheath Hall in 1919, and opened the School of Agriculture there in 1921: its predecessor had been located at Holmes Chapel. This hostel for the women from the Dairy Institute was opened by the Prince of Wales in 1926.

125. An advertisement for Nantwich and Acton Grammar School, 1930. Note that the curriculum took account of the needs of the rural community; also that fees had to be paid. Girls were admitted from 1905.

Leisure & Special Events

126.   The Alexandra Football Club of Crewe is one of the oldest clubs in the league. It was founded in 1876, and entered the second division in 1892. The club is pictured *c*.1886-7.

127. Engine drivers pose here, *c.*1879-80, with the chairman of the L.N.W.R., Sir Richard Moon. He had joined the company board in 1851, became chairman 10 years later, and remained in office until 1891. Moon decided that Crewe Works should become the company's central workshops.

128. This photograph shows railway officials from Siam at Crewe Works in the 19th century. They are standing with the Chief Mechanical Engineer, Francis Webb outside the General Offices and in front of the C.M.E.'s coupé, which was used when inspecting track or locomotives.

129. As early as 1859 army volunteers were recruited at the Works in response to military threats by the French. By 1897,

when this parade in Market Square took place, they were known as the 2nd Cheshire Railway Volunteers.

130. The Volunteers fought in the Boer War of 1899-1902, and the 1935 Veterans Reunion is shown here. Presumably the sole lady present served as a nurse. Volunteer forces were disbanded in 1912, when the Territorial Army was established.

131. In 1913, Crewe Works was visited by royalty. Their Majesties are inspecting a coach that was built for Queen Adelaide, daughter of the duke of Saxe-Meiningen, queen to William IV. The coach must have been one of the earliest produced by Crewe Carriage Works.

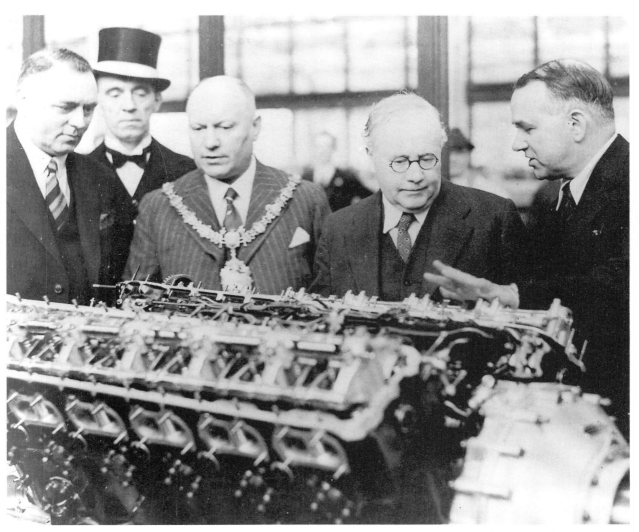

132.   In July 1939 the official opening of the Rolls Royce aero engine factory, by the Air Minister, Sir Kingsley Wood, took place. He is being shown an engine by Ernest Hives, Director of Rolls Royce Ltd. John Morris, the Works Manager, and Harry Bricks, the mayor of Crewe, are also in attendance.

133. King George VI and Queen Elizabeth were assiduous in performing royal duties throughout the Second World War, and the Queen is shown here during their visit to Rolls Royce on 28 August 1940.

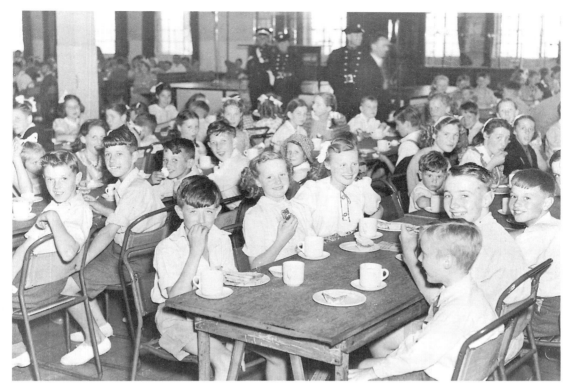

134. Rolls Royce encouraged leisure pursuits and provided sports facilities for its employees. The annual Sports Day included a children's party, pictured in 1948.

135. Coronation decorations on the Rolls Royce offices. After the austerity of the post-war years, this occasion provided an opportunity for relaxation and celebration.

136. In the 19th and early 20th centuries brass and silver bands were very popular. Hassall's band is an example of a town band (photographed in 1898). The Nantwich town band was re-formed in 1983.

137. Nantwich cricket team poses with pride, having won the league in 1954. Today the team plays in the North Staffordshire and South Cheshire league. The most famous president of the club was A. N. Hornby (plate 172).

138.   The Old Wyche Theatre opened in 1919 at the corner of Market Street and Churchyardside, and was Nantwich's first cinema. Before this date magic lantern slides had been shown in the Town Hall. The Ebenezer chapel in Mill Street also was converted into a cinema, and is now a nightclub.

139. On 20 October 1926 the Prince of Wales visited Nantwich. Insisting on riding in the open coupé from Chester he was reportedly in ill humour by the time he arrived, as the day was cold. During his visit the prince opened new buildings at the Cheshire School of Agriculture, Reaseheath Hall.

140. Nantwich Cheese Fair was first held *c*.1820. Farmhouse cheese production peaked in 1907, when 600,000 cwt. was made. Factory production began during the following year. The picture shows Mrs. Maria Lee Good with prizes that she won for cheeses exhibited in 1932.

Businesses & Services

141.   These shops, in Coppenhall Terrace, Crewe, pictured *c.*1930, were built by the L.N.W.R. The tree-lined terrace was a popular evening walk in the town centre.

142. Crewe High Street leads from Edleston Road to Mill Street. The buildings include the offices of the *Crewe Chronicle*, opposite the cinema, which the newspaper has occupied since 1875.

143. *Queen's Hotel*, Station Street, standing alone in 1960 on land that has been cleared of the houses it once served. The building is unpretentious but dignified: the arch perhaps gave access to stabling.

144. The *Earl of Crewe* on the Nantwich Road has a splendid modern sign which depicts the last Earl of Crewe.

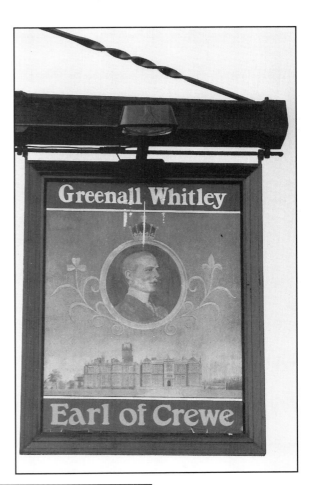

145. High on the gable of the *Earl of Crewe* hotel is this terracotta panel which depicts Queen Victoria surrounded by images of her empire. It commemorates her Diamond Jubilee, and thus dates the building to 1897.

146. Richard Whittle (1820-86) was associated for 36 years with Crewe Co-operative Friendly Society. While mayor in 1880 he presented this lamp standard, in Jubilee Gardens, to the aldermen and burgesses of the borough. Whittle was also a Justice of the Peace.

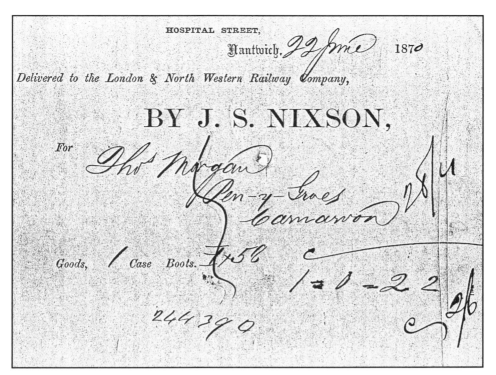

147. This delivery note to the L.N.W.R., dating from 1870, is a reminder that Nantwich was an important centre of boot and shoe manufacture in the 19th century.

148. Advertisement for E. G. and E. H. Steventon, footwear specialists, of Hospital Street, Nantwich.

E. G. & E. H. STEVENTON

Specialists in
WIDE FITTING FOOTWEAR

1a, HOSPITAL STREET, NANTWICH.   'Phone: 5184.

Sole Agents for CLARK'S " TOR," "WAUKEEZI" and "MOCCASIN"
High-class LADIES' AND GENT'S BOOTS AND SHOES.

Also OUR OWN WELL KNOWN "H" BRAND HAND MADE, TO
MEASURE, FOOTWEAR, MADE AT OUR OWN BARKER ST. FACTORY.

REPAIRS of all kinds, collected and delivered.

QUALITY AND SERVICE always our aim.

149. H. Knowles and Son, coal merchants. Coal was an important freight traffic on the railways from their inception in the 19th century. Most stations had facilities to tranship coal for local distribution by road. Nantwich had a medium-sized goods yard with provision for coal bunkers. The only traces left are a former goods shed and a coal merchant's premises.

150. Zan Stores was a company which took over the site of a grocer's shop in Nantwich at the junction of Swine Market and High Street – which became known as Zan site. The company appears to have been in business in the 19th century.

151. In 1859 Philip H. Chester established his grocery shop, pictured here *c*.1910, at the corner of Hospital Street and Pillory Street, Nantwich. These buildings were shortly to be swept away to be replaced by the grand building which still occupies the site. It was designed by the Nantwich firm of Bower and Edleston.

152.   The interior of Chester's Store in 1935. Company policy made provision for apprentices to 'live in' above the store.

153. Municipal gas supplies in England date from the 1820s. Nantwich Gas Works stood off Welsh Row, and the gas department also sold gas fitments. The works hooter was used to summon the rival fire brigades (see plates 156 and 157): one long blast for a country fire and three short blasts for the town.

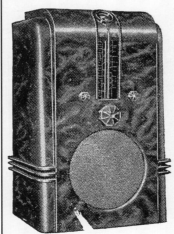
154. Radiomes Ltd., in the late 1920s. By this time the range of wireless sets was impressive and, as their appeal grew, sets became less expensive.

NANTWICH SAVINGS BANK

29, HIGH STREET.

Established 1817. Certified under the Act of 1863.

Total Funds exceed £1,700,000

SAVINGS BANK

BANK

HOURS OF BUSINESS.

MONDAY
10.30 to 12.30
AND
2.0 to 4.30.

THURSDAY
10.30 to 12.30
AND
2.0 to 4.30

SATURDAY
10.30 to 12.30
AND
2.0 to 4.30
AND
5.0 to 7.0 p.m.

This is your Bank.

$3\frac{1}{2}\%$ given on all sums in the Special Investment Department.

Come and open an account for yourself and children. You can start with sixpence. No expense, no trouble, no risk.

GEO. H. HARDING, *Actuary*.

155. The Savings Bank movement originated to provide a service for small investors in the late 18th century: a safe income was guaranteed by the Commissioners of the National Debt. In 1930, only a modest sum was required to open an account, and the bank was open late on Saturdays.

156.   Following the Great Fire in 1583, William Sands provided Nantwich's first firefighting apparatus. Water was pumped from the River Weaver by a waterwheel and directed into the streets through wooden pipes. This photograph of the volunteer fire brigade was taken in 1870.

157. In 1894, Nantwich Urban District Council set up another fire brigade (seen here in 1925). For the early years of this century the two brigades operated in direct competition, even though they shared premises in Market Street.

158. The *Black Lion* in Nantwich was a coaching inn dating from 1664. The simple 'studding' (decoration of the timber) reflects the utilitarian purpose of this building.

159. The name of this pub in Welsh Row, Nantwich, is believed to be a corruption of 'the swan with two nicks' – these being the markings that were cut into the beak to denote ownership.

160. *Bowling Green* Inn was built as a farm on the outskirts of Nantwich in the 15th century, on land owned by Combermere Abbey. Licensed as 'an ale bar only' in 1775, it was only granted a full licence in 1891. The bowling green from which the inn took its name was alongside.

Villages

161. The earliest records of a church in Barthomley date from 1090, but the oldest surviving fabric is the tower, built in the late 15th century. The dedication to St Bertoline, who is said to have performed miracles on this site, is very unusual. Alsager, Balterley, Crewe and Haslington used to be included in the parish. In the church today there are still tombs of the ancient Fouleshurst family, and the fine Crewe chapel, created by Sir Ranulph Crewe.

162. These boards in St Bertoline's church list benefactors to the parish, beginning with Sir Ranulph Crewe in 1672.

163. St Boniface (675-754), to whom the church at Bunbury is dedicated, was an Englishman who became archbishop of Mainz. The church was damaged during the Second World War by enemy action. Recently a medieval panel, painted by itinerant craftsmen, that pictures saints, was reinstated in the south aisle.

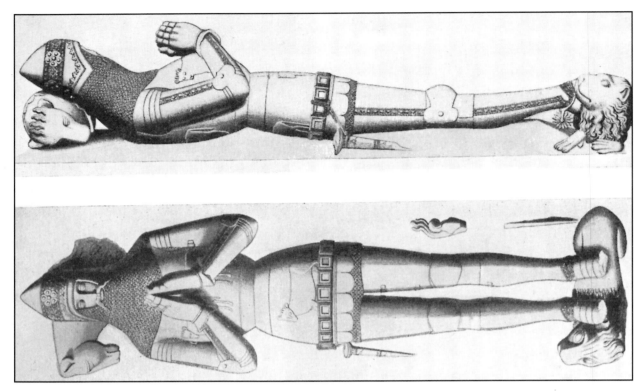

164. Sir Hugh Calveley endowed a college of priests at Bunbury in the 14th century. He spent much of his life fighting in France and may have been buried there when he died in 1394. This is the earliest memorial tomb in Cheshire, and the effigy is made of alabaster. Calveley village on the Chester to Nantwich road is named after Sir Hugh.

165. The Wilbraham tomb at St Mary's, Acton, erected in 1740 by Grace, Countess of Dysart, commemorates Sir Richard Wilbraham, Sir Thomas (his son), and their wives. The effigies are of Sir Thomas and his lady, and provide a good record of fashions of 1660. On the end of the tomb are family shields.

166. The oldest gravestone in Acton churchyard reads 'Here lyeth inte(rred) the body of Rich(ard) Filcock of Cholmondeston who died July the 16 1671'. Cholmondeston is a small village to the east of Acton.

167. Dating from the late 17th century is this 12 ft.-high sundial in Acton churchyard. It is possibly the finest example in Cheshire, although now much decayed. The Latin inscription reads: 'Time flies, death comes: as the hour, so is life'.

168.   In the early medieval period, Acton was as important as Nantwich, but did not grow like its neighbour. Here, in 1905, horse-drawn vehicles await their passengers outside the *Star* Inn. A mounting block on the right and a Dorfold estate cottage complete the scene. Even today the village is little changed.

169. A chantry was established at Acton in the 14th century by the Dorfold family. St Mary's church was rebuilt in the 1890s for the second time, as a storm had demolished the tower and damaged the roof in 1757. Notable tombs of the Mainwaring and Wilbraham families are located here.

170. The church at Church Minshull was once connected with Combermere Abbey and was a chapel of ease of Acton. The wooden building was demolished in 1702 and the present brick building, dedicated to St Bartholomew, replaced it. The villagers were too poor to pay for rebuilding, so were granted a 'brief' to allow collections for it throughout the realm.

171. John Gerard (1545-1612) was born in Nantwich and educated at Wistaston. His herbal of 1597 was the first to use English names for medicinal plants. For example, he refers to 'raspis [blackberries] growing on the causeway at Wistaston'. Gerard became a surgeon in London where he was also a superintendent of Gardens to Lord Burghley, Lord Treasurer of England.

172.   Albert Neilson Hornby was the son of the M.P. for Blackburn, but lived in the Nantwich area for much of his life – for a time at Church Minshull – and he is buried at Acton. Hornby played rugby and cricket for England, thus becoming known as 'the cricketing squire'. He was also a Conservative county councillor and a Beam Heath trustee.

173.   Hornby played for the M.C.C. in the 1877 centennial match against England. He also captained England in the 1882 test series against Australia when the home country lost the Oval Test and the Ashes of English cricket were laid to rest. Subsequently, Hornby was President of Lancashire County Cricket Club for 20 years. His grave in Acton churchyard is pictured: the epitaph is appropriate for a great cricketer.

174. A church was in existence in Wybunbury in the 13th century. All that remains today is the 15th-century tower. The rest of the building was demolished in 1978 as streams on the hillside were undermining the fabric. Memorials to the Smith of Hough and Delves families stood in the aisles: the former is now relocated at St Mary's, Nantwich. The church was dedicated to St Chad, a Celtic bishop of Lichfield.